MARY
CASSATT

MARY CASSATT

An Amercian in Paris

BY PHILIP BROOKS

A FIRST BOOK

FRANKLIN WATTS
NEW YORK / CHICAGO / LONDON / TORONTO / SYDNEY

Frontispiece: *Young Women Picking Fruit*, 1891, oil on canvas, 51½ x 35½ in.

Cover photographs copyright ©: Dallas Museum of Art, Munger Fund, 1952.38.M, Mary Cassatt, *Sleepy Baby*, c. 1910, pastel on paper, 25½ x 20½; Mary Cassatt, carte-de-visite, albumen print, ca. 1872, Baroni and Gardelli photographers. Courtesy of the Pennsylvania Academy of the Fine Arts, Philadelphia. Archives. (detail) (inset)

Photographs copyright ©: Carnegie Museum of Art, Pittsburgh, Patron's Art Fund, 22.8: p. 2; The National Portrait Gallery, Smithsonian Institution: p. 8; Memorial Art Gallery of the University of Rochester, Marion Stratton Gould Fund: p. 11; Art Resource, N.Y.: pp. 13, 43 (both Bridgeman), 30, 31 (both Scala), 35, 49 (both Giraudon); North Wind Picture Archives: pp. 15, 19, 21, 24; Frederick A. Sweet Papers, Archives of American Art, Smithsonian Institution: pp. 17, 60; Pennsylvania Academy of the Fine Arts, Philadelphia, Archives, photo by Gihon and Rixon: p. 22; The Art Institute of Chicago: pp. 27 (Solomon A. Smith Fund, 1965.8), 51 (Mr. and Mrs. Martin A. Ryerson Collection, 1932.1289), 52 (Robert A. Waller Fund, 1910.2); Sterling and Francine Clark Art Institute, Williamstown, Massachusetts: p. 32; The Hayden Collection, courtesy of Museum of Fine Arts, Boston: p. 38; Board of Trustees, National Gallery of Art, Washington, © 1994: pp. 40 (Collection of Mr. and Mrs. Paul Mellon), 47 (Chester Dale Collection), 56 (Chester Dale Collection); Philadelphia Museum of Art, The W. P. Wilstach Collection: p. 46; Virginia Museum of Fine Arts, Richmond, Va., Museum Purchase, with funds provided by anonymous donor: p. 54; Knoedler Gallery, New York: p. 59.

Library of Congress Cataloging-in-Publication Data

Brooks, Philip, 1963–
Mary Cassatt: an American in Paris / by Philip Brooks.
p. cm. — (A First book)
Includes bibliographical references and index.
ISBN 0-531-20183-X
1. Cassatt, Mary, 1844–1926—Juvenile literature. 2. Expatriate painters—France—Paris—Biography—Juvenile literature. 3. Painters—United States—Biography—Juvenile literature. [1. Cassatt, Mary, 1844–1926. 2. Artists. 3. Women—Biography.] I. Title. II. Series.
ND237.C3B76 1995
[B]   759.13—dc20   94-41482 CIP AC

CONTENTS

MARY CASSATT: AN AMERICAN IN PARIS

*T*am not willing to accept that a woman can draw that well!" That's what the artist Edgar Degas said after seeing one of Mary Cassatt's pictures. It was the year 1891, and Degas's attitude was a common one in Paris and around the world.

Today, there are many well-known women artists. But when Mary Cassatt was a girl, in the mid-nineteenth century, very few of the world's famous art schools admitted young women. Those that did often separated them from the young men studying there. Women were not allowed into classes where male artists learned how to draw and sculpt the human body by looking at nude models. It was thought a proper woman should not see such things! Women were not even welcome at social gatherings where male artists discussed new ideas and techniques.

**Mary Cassatt, *a self-portrait, 1880,*
*watercolor on paper, 13 x 9⅝ in.***

Mary's early childhood was spent in Pennsylvania, in traditional communities where, in those days, girls were taught to play the piano, paint china, or draw. This training was not intended to prepare them to become serious artists, but to produce refined young ladies who would make good marriages and become good wives.

Tradition and the "rules" of society were considered more important in northeastern American cities in the 1840s and 1850s than they are today. People tended to attach significance to social class. Money, property, and influence gave some families status. Others were honored because their ancestors had been rich and powerful for as long as anyone could remember. When Mary's father became very successful through business investments, he hoped to be welcomed and respected by those men and women who had been born into wealth, power, and honor. He wanted his children to be secure and respected, also. Perhaps this is why, when Mary told him of her wish to go to Paris to study to become an artist, he furiously replied, as Mary later told a biographer, "I would almost rather see you dead!"

Mr. Cassatt argued that being a professional artist was not respectable. Painting was a career for men, and these men were not necessarily of the best character. Further, there were certain things well-brought-up girls did not do. They did not travel alone in the nineteenth century! They did not sail off to Europe to become painters! What would people think?

Mary loved her father and wanted to please him. In fact, she wanted to please everyone. But she loved to paint more than anything she could possibly imagine doing. Her passion for art was more important to her than doing the "proper" thing. So a day came when she packed her trunks and suitcases and prepared to cross the ocean, to go to Europe where she could begin to work toward her goal.

Mary would overcome the artistic problems faced by every aspiring artist, in addition to the obstacles placed in her way by a male-dominated art world. Few male painters accepted her as a colleague. She lived abroad and, for long periods, far from her family. She never married or had children, and often faced loneliness, jealousy, and a lack of understanding.

Today, Mary's magnificent paintings, drawings, and prints hang in the world's great museums. When museum-goers stand before a Mary Cassatt picture, most of them do not really care whether a man or woman created what they see. They absorb the beauty of the colors, the delicate grace of the lines, the way light seems to glow from the canvas.

In one sense, however, it does matter that Mary Cassatt was a woman painter. What Mary did was heroic. Her life's work helped to change ideas about women in the arts. Many talented women before Mary Cassatt might never have realized their potential because of concern with being "respectable" or "lady-like." In time, even Mary's father grew to understand her ambition and came to believe she

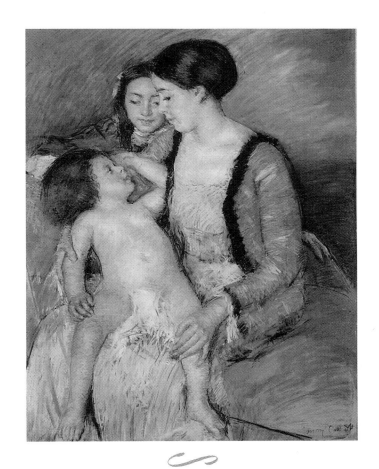

Young Mother, Daughter and Baby,
pastel on paper, 43¼ x 33¼ in.

had made the right choices in her life. He became very proud of his daughter's accomplishments and argued in her defense against those who said she had no place in the "man's world" of art.

one

A SPIRITED GIRL

ary's determination even when faced with obstacles could be seen when she was very young. She was born on May 22, 1844, in Allegheny City (now a part of Pittsburgh), Pennsylvania, and was named Mary Stevenson Cassatt. Even as a little girl she was independent and demanding. Her temper was quick and her tantrums were notable. She screamed, cried, and kicked until she got her way—to the annoyance of her brothers and sisters. There were five Cassatt children: Lydia, Alexander (called Aleck), Robert (Robbie), Mary, the fourth child, and Gardner, born five years after Mary. Like most brothers and sisters, the Cassatt children had occasional fights—especially Aleck and Mary. But, as Aleck later wrote, they soon were friends again.

Katherine Cassatt, Mary's mother, was an educated, intelligent woman with opinions on politics and

Reading Le Figaro *by Mary Cassatt. This portrait of her mother reading a newspaper was painted in Paris, about 1883.*

current events. In this period, women were generally expected to be rather quiet in public, and to let their husbands speak for them. Katherine Cassatt was not quiet but outgoing, and she made many friends. She had traveled abroad and could speak and read French very well. Mary loved her and was proud of her. Mary's father, Robert, a strong-willed and accomplished man himself, was also proud of his wife. *Reading Le Figaro*, 1883, is a portrait of Katherine Cassatt.

Mary loved her father, too. But, as she grew up, she was in awe of him. He was a business investor, had been the mayor of Allegheny City, and seemed to know everything. With a forceful personality, he always seemed able to take control of a situation. He was also mysterious. One never knew quite what he was thinking. Mary imagined she would never be able to do anything as well as her father did it.

When Mary was five, her father moved the family to a new house he'd built in Philadelphia. Katherine and Robert Cassatt wanted to be accepted into Philadelphia society. They also looked for the business, cultural, and educational opportunities of a big city. However, within a few years, the Cassatts were moving again.

In 1851, Robert Cassatt decided to take his family to live in Europe for a while. America was still a very new country and lacking in traditional learning. Katherine and Robert Cassatt and their contemporaries believed that most of what was great in human culture, and important to see and know about, still lay across the ocean in Europe. A long stay abroad, they hoped, would allow the young Cassatts to become educated, well mannered, and cultured.

Philadelphia in the mid-nineteenth century was a busy city with private clubs, cultural activities, and society balls at the Assembly building.

All the Cassatt children would benefit from their time in Europe, studying in European schools, learning French and other languages, and gaining a broader view of the world. However, it was Mary who would be most influenced by her time abroad.

two

EUROPE

In the summer of 1851, the Cassatts visited London. After about a month they moved on to France, where they were to live for nearly two years.

Once settled in a comfortable apartment in Paris, the Cassatt children were taken almost immediately to the Louvre (LOO-vruh). The Louvre is one of the largest and most famous art museums in the world. Among the almost countless masterpieces in the Louvre's collection is the *Mona Lisa*, painted by the Italian artist Leonardo da Vinci. The Cassatts visited many other important art museums and galleries in the city, too. The children attended French schools and mastered the French language. They ate at fine restaurants and attended the many cultural activities of the great capital city.

In 1853, the Cassatts moved to Germany—first to Heidelberg, and then Darmstadt. Aleck, Mary's older brother, showed great promise as an engineer, and their father wanted him to attend a respected technical school in the city of Darmstadt.

The opportunity for Aleck to get fine training was not the only reason the Cassatts moved to Germany. Mary's brother Robbie was suffering from a mysterious bone disease, and the family hoped to consult several renowned German doctors. However, the bone disease worsened, and the doctors were unable to help. Robbie died. Mary was eleven years old, and Robbie—just two years older—had been her closest companion in the family.

A few months after Robbie's funeral, the Cassatts, grieving and homesick, went back to America. Aleck stayed in Germany to finish his engineering studies.

An 1854 engraving of a family scene in Heidelberg shows Gardner (left), Robbie, and Mary, with their father.

three

~

SEEING THE SALON

The family interrupted their trip home with a stop in Paris, where they spent time viewing "the Salon." The Salon was an annual art competition sponsored by the French government. Each year, artists submitted works to a jury that made selections to be included in the Salon exhibition, and awarded ribbons and medals to those they judged the best. All of Paris toured the exhibition and argued over which pictures and sculptures were good, and which were so terrible they should never have been shown in public. In France, art was an important part of the country's daily life, and most people had strong opinions about it. In Paris, the art center of the world in this period, artists' ideas were discussed and argued about in the same way Americans discussed and argued over political questions.

Life on the Paris boulevards in the 1870s,
where art was a topic of everyday discussion

Mary was impressed by this aspect of life in France, as well as by the art she saw at the Salon. It was at this time that art began to have great importance in her life. The Salon competition, also, was to be significant in her efforts to become an artist.

During the next five years, living near or in Philadelphia, Pennsylvania, Mary's enthusiasm and eagerness to study art increased. At fifteen, she later told biographers, she knew that all she wanted was to be an artist. And she was willing to work as hard as necessary to be one. She knew she'd have to overcome added problems because she was a woman, but she was confident and determined. And fortunately, the art world had begun to open its doors a little bit wider for women.

By 1859, most American art schools were accepting some women students, although they still studied under different conditions than did their male peers. While young men were learning to draw and sculpt the human body using nude models, the young women in life-drawing classes might have a live horse or cow to draw instead. They saw only old plaster casts of the human body.

Mary had to wait until she was sixteen to be accepted at an art school. Finally, she was able to begin, with a first class in "drawing from the antique" at the Pennsylvania Academy of the Fine Arts in Philadelphia. Mary and the other young women at the Academy saw themselves as pioneers, but they were still limited by old attitudes and customs, including styles of dress. They wore elaborate clothes, with long skirts and puffed sleeves that were often spattered with paint or ink and coated with dust from plaster and marble.

From 1860 to 1862, Mary attended the Academy, learning the basic technical skills of drawing. She became restless and impatient with the program—drawing endless pictures of plaster casts of human hands, for instance, and attending long lectures on human anatomy. She was eager to begin

The "Antique Class" at the Pennsylvania Academy of the Fine Arts, in the 1870s, where art students worked from classical sculptures

painting, and began working on her own. For two more years she continued with some classes at the Academy and studied painting privately.

She spent this period—during which the country was divided by the bitter Civil War—studying at the Academy, working from local models, copying masterworks at Philadelphia museums and galleries, and sharing ambitions and dreams with Eliza Haldeman, a classmate at the Academy who had become a close friend. Mary longed for what she'd glimpsed in Paris. Art seemed to be really important there, a part of life. She felt that she had learned all she could from her teachers in Philadelphia and now needed to study the great paintings in the Louvre's collection.

As the Civil War ended in 1865, Mary began to consider how best to achieve her goal of becoming a real artist. She believed she needed to take a bold step to achieve what she wanted, and that Paris held her destiny. Despite the loud protestations of her father, who'd hoped she would settle down, marry a wealthy young man, and have a family, Mary packed and, with her mother accompanying her, took a ship across the Atlantic Ocean to Paris. A few months later Eliza Haldeman and some other students from the Academy followed, for Paris was a magnet that seemed to draw all young artists.

Mary Cassatt (right) and Eliza Haldeman (left),
with other students and a friend at the
Pennsylvania Academy of the Fine Arts, 1862

four

IN PARIS

Mary was soon disillusioned after she arrived in Paris. The École des Beaux-Arts, France's most important art academy, did not accept women. This made Mary angry, but she did not give up her dream of studying art in Paris.

Mary learned that women artists could get along quite well without the Beaux-Arts. They discussed ideas among themselves, copied master paintings and drawings in the Louvre, and were able to take private lessons from teachers at the École des Beaux-Arts. When Mary was accepted as a student by one of the most popular painting masters in Paris, Jean-Léon Gérôme, her fellow students in Paris and in Philadelphia (where the news spread quickly) were impressed. Women also formed informal groups and schools and learned about the important artists of the day by attending Salon exhibitions.

The Louvre Museum, Paris, where Mary and other young artists spent hours copying and studying old masters

Yet Mary still felt excluded by the established art world in Paris. It felt stuffy, old-fashioned, and unfair. She and Eliza Haldeman had similar feelings. They were tired of being treated as inferior to male artists. Instead of simply complaining or giving up, however, they decided to move outside that established world.

In 1867 the two young women went to see, and stayed in artists' colonies in the villages of France. They spent their days painting pictures of beautiful rolling fields where peasants planted and harvested their food. This type of painting, of peasants and everyday village life, was very popular in Paris. Some artists specialized in these pastoral, or "genre," paintings and made a good living.

Mary and Eliza worked hard, and in 1868 were rewarded when both had paintings accepted for that year's Salon competition. Mary's painting was of a young peasant girl playing a mandolin.

Few women artists had paintings exhibited in the Salon. The judges usually were conservative old men. Mary believed this was the first real encouragement she'd ever gotten and she hoped now, that with time and hard work, she would be fully accepted as an artist in Paris.

Eliza Haldeman returned to the United States in December 1868. In 1870, after five years abroad, Mary too sailed back to the United States. France had just ended a bitter war with Prussia, which was then a powerful military nation in central Europe. The French government had been weakened by the long war. Civil unrest was commonplace in Paris and in the countryside. Mary's family begged her to come home. She reluctantly returned to Philadelphia.

five

BACK HOME

After so much time away, Mary found Philadelphia pleasantly familiar, and she was glad to see her family. Still, she missed Europe, despite her frustration with the tradition-bound art world. In Paris, she'd left behind a community of women artists who supported and encouraged each other, and from whom she'd learned a great deal.

At home, her studio space was cramped and dark. The paints and brushes she preferred were manufactured in Europe, and she could not get them in America. Even more, she felt she needed to be close to the great art that filled Europe's museums and exhibition halls. And she needed the fields and peasants she'd painted with such affection and success. It was not that she "liked" France better than Philadelphia. Nearly all painters find a place that comes to belong to them, a place that captures their imagination completely. Her trip home convinced her that she had to be in France in order to create.

While longing to return to Europe, Mary tried to continue working. Lacking the peasants and village scenes she liked, she started a portrait of her father. He was a poor model, as he tended to fall asleep while posing. But this began Mary's interest in painting portraits of family members. In her many later paintings of her mother, father, or sister, Lydia, one can sense the artist's deep connection to her subject.

Her Father Reading
c. 1881, graphite sketch by Mary Cassatt

Mary was very eager to sell her work. Her goal was to be a professional artist, able to support herself. She put together a collection of her best work and took it to art dealers and collectors in Philadelphia, Boston, and New York. No one seemed interested in her paintings. She decided to try Chicago. She left her work in an art shop there and returned to Philadelphia. Just a few days later, the Great Chicago Fire of 1871—started, according to popular history, when a cow kicked over a lantern!—burned nearly the entire city to the ground. Mary's paintings were destroyed.

Things were not going well for Mary in America. Still, there was nothing to do but to keep painting, drawing, and hoping to return to France.

As if to answer her wish, a letter soon arrived from a Catholic bishop in Pittsburgh. He wanted copies of two religious paintings by the Italian master Correggio, who had lived in the early sixteenth century, to place in his cathedral. The paintings were from a church in Parma, Italy. The bishop offered to pay Mary a good sum of money to travel to Parma and make copies of the paintings. Here was the opportunity the twenty-seven-year-old aspiring artist had been waiting for! Without hesitation, she packed her trunk, said her good-byes, and left for Italy.

six

ITALY

In Parma, Mary enthusiastically set to work copying Correggio's glowing, 350-year-old paintings, and studying the artist's techniques. She was happy to be in an art community again, and to be able to see great old masters in Parma's museums and churches. She traveled to other Italian towns and cities and saw countless paintings of the Madonna and baby Jesus. Mary was inspired by these images of mother and child. Later she would paint many pictures of mothers and their babies.

Correggio had covered the church ceilings with paintings of angels who were shown not as solemn religious figures, but as frolicking, joyful children. A sweetness and beautiful light shone from the work. Mary copied the two pictures she'd been commissioned to do and also sketched nearly every image she

In Parma, Mary studied the vibrant
sixteenth-century works of Correggio.

found in the church—human figures from every angle
and in various poses. She worked to find out just how
Correggio achieved the magical effects that moved her
so deeply hundreds of years after his death.

   Correggio used a technique called shading—
darkening certain areas of a figure to make the body
appear more rounded, more three-dimensional. He
also used the way light fell on the faces and bodies

of the figures in his pictures to make them more dramatic. Sometimes his people looked like actors under a spotlight on a dark stage. Mary studied the way he used this dramatic technique to make his viewers feel sadness or religious exaltation.

From Italy, Mary took a number of trips to Spain. There she studied the works of the great Spanish painters Velázquez, Goya, and Murillo. She traveled to the countryside and painted genre pictures of Spanish peasant life. In these paintings, one can see the influence of Velázquez and Goya in the

During visits to Spain, Mary studied the works of Murillo, who often painted scenes of peasant life, and those of other Spanish masters.

way she applied paint to the canvas. These Spanish masters used thicker globs and dollops of paint than she'd been taught to use. This gave their pictures more texture, creating the feeling that one could walk into the scene they showed.

Like Correggio, Spanish painters used dramatic lighting in their work, often placing brightly lit figures against very dark backgrounds to make the subjects stand out from the canvas and almost glow. This Spanish influence is seen in works such as *Offering the Panale to the Bullfighter*, which Mary painted in 1873.

Offering the Panale to the Bullfighter, 1873, oil on canvas, 39⅝ x 33½ in.

seven

A RETURN TO PARIS

Throughout her life, Mary always felt drawn to France. Paris was difficult. The streets were crowded, noisy, and dirty. Petty arguments turned into huge debates. Artists were rejected by galleries because they were women, or didn't know the right people, or said the wrong thing to the wrong person. But, Mary knew, despite all these things, that Paris was still the best place to learn about art and the best place to sell paintings. And these were the two passions of her life.

In 1873 she returned to Paris. By now, Mary's work was well known in France. Although genre painting no longer interested her as much as her other work, she was able to sell her genre pictures fairly quickly. She made enough money to buy food, paints, and brushes, and to pay her rent. Still, her work did not sell as well in America. When one or two paintings were bought by American collectors, she was very happy. She considered herself an American, and wanted other Americans to appreciate her art. Also, she wanted to become well known in the United States to make her father proud of her.

In spite of her success with the French public, the judges at the annual Salon were less enthusiastic about her paintings. The men who judged the contest looked for the same thing in every picture set before them: balance of composition, clarity, a highly polished style. Artists like Mary, who were beginning to experiment with a new, freer style of painting, found themselves kept out of the Salon.

Mary did not wish to change the way she painted just to win awards. A few of her pictures were accepted, but often the judges said her colors were too bright and her brushstrokes too choppy and fluttery.

Mary disagreed. Although she felt many works of the past were brilliant, she thought they were just that—works of the past. She felt something new had to be done, something had to be added to the traditions handed down by the old masters.

One reason many painters were searching for something new was that photography had recently been invented. Painters were no longer needed to record what a person or object looked like. Photographs could achieve that much better and faster than painting on canvas could. Mary and some other painters saw this change as a good thing. Painters were now free to do all kinds of things never before explored.

This spirit of adventure was what Mary found in the work of the French artist Edgar Degas. He was ten years older than Mary, and was closer to having found his own way of expressing himself. It is hard for us today to imagine how stunning his work must have been for a public used to the sedate colors and

Degas's pastels, filled with color and energy, opened a new direction for Mary.

classical composition used by painters for hundreds of years. Mary saw his drawings for the first time in an art dealer's window. Degas had worked with colored chalks called "pastels." She stopped and stared at the drawings. They seemed to vibrate with bright color, the energy of frantic-looking lines, and scribbles of pink, yellow, purple, blue, and red. Never had she seen anything on paper that was so filled with movement! His composition placed subjects at strange angles and in unusual or informal poses. Mary found herself drawn back again and again to look at these drawings.

Degas would later feel the same excitement when he saw one of Cassatt's early paintings, *Ida*, a portrait of a woman, at the Salon of 1874. Degas stood before the painting a long time and said finally, "There is someone who feels as I do!" He was shocked—and a little disappointed at first—to find that a woman had painted the picture.

eight

THE INDEPENDENTS

In 1877, the Salon rejected Mary's work. When Degas heard of this he visited her in her studio. He was by then an established artist. They sat together and had tea. Degas told her that she was right not to change her brushstrokes or her beautiful, bright colors to please the Salon judges. He invited her to show her work with a group of artists who had banded together under the name "the Independents."

The Independents would not submit their work to the Salon but mounted their own exhibitions. The Salon, they believed, was in the hands of people with no sense of art as a living thing that grew and changed with time.

Mary faced a difficult choice: the invitation from the Independents offered freedom from the criticisms and restrictions of the Salon judges. But Mary wanted to sell her work, to be successful and become famous. The surest way to achieve that was to be included regularly in the Salon exhibitions. Mary bravely realized she had to be true to herself. Her art would get better only if she felt free to draw and paint as she wanted. She joined the Independents and

At the Opera, *1879, oil on canvas, 31½ x 25½ in.,* is one of Mary's early works showing the influence of the Independents.

never had she felt happier or more excited. It was as if she'd just begun to live!

The Independents were developing a new way to think about painting. Painters of the past had been concerned with the careful posing of a subject, with the creation of a balanced composition, and with perfecting their technique so that their brushstrokes would be nearly invisible. The Independents tried instead to bring a feeling of spontaneity to their canvases, the sense that the person or people in a painting had been caught off guard, completely themselves. The Independents wanted the feeling you find in a candid photograph. They used choppy, squiggly, and feathery brushstrokes to give a sense of vibrant light. They composed a picture trying to catch the viewer's eye in any way possible, with figures in the near foreground or seen from odd angles. Parts of figures or objects might be cut off by the picture's frame, as in a photograph.

These ideas influenced one of Cassatt's early masterpieces, *Little Girl in a Blue Armchair*. Like a candid photograph, the painting looks unposed. The girl sprawls in a chair as little girls really do. Although the child is clearly the subject of the painting, she is not the center of the picture. She appears close to the front of the picture's space. Other chairs and couches are in the background, just as they would appear in a

Little Girl in a Blue Armchair, *1878,*
oil on canvas, 35½ x 51⅛ in.

photograph of a real room. The picture looks "flattened out," the way photographs look.

Mary's ideas about art were always changing and evolving. She looked always for the "best" way to paint what she saw and felt.

nine

CASSATT, DEGAS, AND THE "IMPRESSIONISTS"

Cassatt and Degas became close friends. Theirs was a friendship based on respect for each other's work and critical abilities. Degas was an established master. Cassatt's strong, quick mind challenged his creativity. He did the same for her. She trusted his judgment as she trusted no one else's but her own. When he saw her working on *Little Girl in a Blue Armchair* in her studio, he told her the treatment of the central figure was good, but that areas of the background needed reworking. Mary trusted his judgment and talent so deeply, she even allowed him to pick up a brush and rework part of her canvas.

Cassatt, Degas, and the other Independents continued to work toward a new way of painting, striving to expand the possibilities. They used choppy brushstrokes and gave their subjects an unposed look. They tried to capture a fleeting moment, much as a snapshot does.

Conservative critics did not like their new ideas, claiming the paintings looked sloppy and unfinished. One writer said that such paintings were "nothing but impressions." The Independents now had a new name: the "Impressionists."

Together, the Impressionists changed people's conception of how to paint and how to look at paintings. They used thousands of tiny brushstrokes, dabs, dots, blobs, and squiggles of many colors which, when seen from a distance, blended to form one color, one figure, or landscape. They saw that shadows were never really black, but were a dark purple color. They painted them that way.

Mary began experimenting with different materials. She started using pastels—the colored chalks of Degas's drawings—to sketch in the new "impressionistic" style.

Cassatt and Degas experimented further with pastels. They mixed them with oil and turpentine to make the colors look richer and brighter, more like paint than chalk. They even steamed their drawings to see if the colors would sink deeper into the paper.

Cassatt's drawings and paintings from this period, often of a woman at the opera or theater, show how Mary's way of seeing the world and drawing it were changing. In *The Theatre Box*, the countless lines and scribbles, in many colors, make up the women's yellow dresses, skin, and hair. The brushstrokes, col-

The Theatre Box

ors, and the figure's casual pose are important features of this painting. The woman seems not to notice she's being painted. She is simply being herself. Looking at the picture, one can get a feeling for her personality, the way she moved, sat, talked.

Mary felt very close to her sister, Lydia, and in some pictures, used her as a model. She was happy when, in 1877, Lydia and the rest of the Cassatt family returned to live in Paris. However, around this time Lydia was diagnosed as having Bright's disease, a kidney ailment. She gradually weakened, and in 1882 she died. Mary was filled with grief and for months was unable to paint. Lydia had been her model, her friend, and her loving sister. Mary's work no longer seemed important to her. With time, she returned to her easel and produced wonderful pictures. But she would never again be so happy and productive as she was during those first months together again with her family, when she'd painted Lydia at the opera or weaving at her loom.

While Mary Cassatt was too sad to find much pleasure in it, the public had at last fully accepted her work. A well-known art dealer, Paul Durand-Ruel, sold her paintings easily in France. Critics who had once scorned her work now praised it. She had not changed her way of painting, but they had changed their way of looking at art. Once a rebellious outsider, she'd become fashionable. The world had changed.

ten

REFINING HER WORK

Cassatt was becoming a more confident and stronger artist. She concentrated on trying to show people as unaware they were being looked at and painted.

In *Woman and Child Driving* (1881), the riders watch the road ahead instead of looking at the viewer. The little girl's hand rests casually on the carriage's fender. The moment seems perfectly simple and natural, but it is a compelling scene. A good example of Cassatt's ability to capture a moment is *Girl Arranging Her Hair*, painted in 1886. An adolescent girl, not particularly beautiful or carefully posed, becomes, in Cassatt's picture, filled with mystery. One wonders what the girl is thinking as she gazes off, daydreaming, her mouth slightly open. This painting was one of Degas's favorites. He traded Mary one of his pastels for the portrait and kept it in his home until he died.

Woman and Child Driving, *1881, oil on canvas,*
35¼ x 51½ in. Lydia, Mary's sister, is pictured
driving a horse-drawn carriage.

Mary became famous for her ability to paint mothers and children as they really were. Her pictures were tender, but not sweet or sentimental. The children she painted were always themselves, whether playing alone, or sharing a moment with their mothers. Family members, including an array of young nieces and nephews, and friends' children were frequent models. Cassatt also painted portraits—enjoying the income they produced. But in these works, too, she placed her subjects in everyday, casual surroundings and worked to achieve an unposed look.

Mary's work was now highly sought. She sold pictures to collectors in America and Europe. It was especially satisfying for her to see Americans becoming interested in owning works of art. She helped collectors who purchased her work to see the paintings of other impressionists, too. Years earlier she had

Girl Arranging Her Hair, *1886, oil on canvas, 29⅝ x 24⅝ in.*

befriended Louisine Elder, a wealthy young American who was a frequent visitor to Paris. Louisine had a great love for and understanding of art, and began to buy works by Cassatt, Degas, Monet, Renoir, and other painters who were creating art in a new way. In 1883, Louisine married Harry Havemeyer, and the couple, with Cassatt as adviser, built a collection of the best work of the time. The Havemeyers left their collection to the Metropolitan Museum of Art in New York City, where it can be seen today. Other wealthy American collectors also sought Cassatt's advice. The paintings she recommended were beautiful, and quickly rose in monetary value. Partly thanks to Mary Cassatt, many works of the Impressionists and other painters of a very exciting period in art history are now in dozens of American museums. Today, American artists and art lovers are able to see great paintings without going all the way to Paris.

And Mary continued working. She began more and more to narrow her subject matter. She painted many pictures of mothers with their young children. Perhaps this had roots in her love for the Italian paintings of the Madonna and child she'd seen in Parma. In painting after painting, Mary shows the strength of the mother-and-child bond. The expressions of her subjects, and the way they hold each other, are beautifully tender.

Mother Holding a Child in Her Arms

eleven

NEW PROJECTS

Mary never stopped learning about art. She and Degas attended an 1890 exhibition of wood-block prints from Japan. The prints were simple and elegant.

Soon, Mary began making prints of her own. Printmaking is very different from drawing or painting, although the artist needs many of the same skills. Printmaking is a complex process requiring patience and great care. First lines and shapes are scratched onto metal plates. Separate plates are used for each color.

The artist works on the plates through a number of steps until they are inked and pressed onto paper. Each plate, with its different-colored ink, adds a layer to the picture until, finally, an image like *In the Omnibus* (1891) is created.

The picture shows the influence of the Japanese style of drawing and printmaking. The picture looks "flat." It doesn't seem that you could walk around in the tram car in the picture. Your eye is drawn to the way the lines move and the simple shapes. The woman seated on the left seems to have Asian features.

Mary Cassatt made only ten different prints during her life. They were difficult to make, and the work was slow and tiring. She was, however, proud of her prints, and considered them among her most important work.

In the Omnibus, 1891, drypoint, soft-ground, and aquatint print

The Bath, *1891, oil on canvas, 39½ x 26 in.*

Some of the same Japanese influences—the use of various patterns on clothing, rugs, and wallpaper, and the flattened-out look of the composition—are evident in what has become Mary Cassatt's best-known painting. *The Bath* was finished around the same time as *In the Omnibus*. The colors are darker than in her earlier work, and richer. It is among the favorite paintings of visitors to the Art Institute of Chicago.

Mary was now one of the most respected artists of her time. In 1891, she had a one-person exhibition at the Durand-Ruel gallery, one of Paris's best galleries.

Soon, she was presented with another honor. A world's fair was to be held in Chicago in 1893 and she was asked, as America's most important woman painter, to paint a huge mural for one of the exposition halls, the Woman's Building. The painting was to portray all types of women in modern society.

Cassatt was living in a large house fifty miles outside of Paris. She built a huge new studio to work in. She designed a three-part mural, each part showing a different aspect of the modern woman. The large center section was *Young Women Plucking the Fruits of Knowledge or Science*. The left panel was *Young Girls Pursuing Fame*, and the right panel was *Arts, Music, Dancing*.

Mary finished the project and shipped it to Chicago. Later, she was angry to find it had been hung forty feet above the ground. Few viewers could see the intricate work she'd done. When the fair was over, all the buildings were destroyed. The mural was lost. Only a few photographs remain of the actual paintings, but Mary kept her preliminary sketches. She had also made several full paintings of subjects that were parts of the huge mural. *Baby Reaching for an Apple* (1893) is thought to be one such study.

Baby Reaching for an Apple, *1893, oil on canvas, 39½ x 25¾ in., is thought to have been inspired by the* Modern Woman *mural Cassatt painted for the Chicago World's Fair.*

twelve

AMERICA

Cassatt's experience with the world's fair mural seemed typical of her luck in America. Despite all her efforts, she was still better known and respected in Europe than in her home country.

When her Paris art dealer decided to open a gallery in New York, Mary eagerly accepted his offer of a one-person show. She worked hard and long to finish new paintings. The exhibit would include one of her largest and most ambitious works, *The Boating Party*. The subject was again a mother and her child. This is one of Mary's few paintings where a man— perhaps a father—is present as well. Both mother and child seem to be gazing into the man's eyes. The picture is full of movement. The man's dark clothing contrasts with the yellow boat and light clothing of the mother and child. Again, we can see the influ-

The Boating Party, *1894*,
oil on canvas, 35⁷⁄₁₆ x 46⅛ in.

ence of Japanese prints. The picture looks flat and is made up of simple shapes and colors.

Unfortunately, American critics of the time did not care much for *The Boating Party* or any of Mary

Cassatt's other paintings. They had not seen as much "impressionistic" work as had the European critics who were now praising her painting. They said the paintings were "somewhat crude" and "unfinished." Few pictures were sold. Mary felt herself a failure—despite her many successes and the popular and critical praise she had earned throughout her career.

This was the beginning of a bad time for Mary. Much of her trouble stemmed from grief over the deaths of the remaining members of her family—her father, her mother, and her brother Aleck. When her youngest brother, Gardner, died, she became terribly depressed and suffered a nervous and physical breakdown. She did not paint or draw for nearly a year. She was too tired and sad to work.

She began to work again in 1912, but there was more hardship. Her eyesight began to fail. She was found to have diabetes, a disease which in those days sometimes led to blindness. Doctors found cataracts in her eyes and she lost most of her vision. Despite all she'd achieved in her life, she became a bitter, disappointed, and unhappy person.

thirteen

MORE
HARDSHIP

In 1914, World War I broke out. The German army invaded France, and Mary was forced to leave her home in the French countryside and move to Paris. A show of her paintings alongside Degas's included the last work of her life. She did not abandon art, but continued trying to help artists she admired. She worked to sell her own paintings in the United States and mounted solo exhibitions in Paris and New York. Near the end of her life, her work became, at last, popular among Americans. This was her final satisfaction.

After Degas's death in 1917, Mary felt isolated and alone. She often felt ill and was quarrelsome and difficult. She continued to work, however, first with a writer on her biography, then on a book-length study of her work. She also traveled extensively.

In 1915, New York's Knoedler Gallery presented a "Loan Exhibition of Masterpieces by Old and Modern Masters," showing works by Edgar Degas (to the right of the doorway) and Mary Cassatt (to the left).

Mary Cassatt was awarded many honors, including the French Legion of Honor. This medal was rarely given to a woman, much less one from America!

By 1921, she was nearly blind. She died five years later, at Château de Beaufresne, the country home she had bought in 1893. She was eighty-two.

Some years later, the United States post office produced two stamps to honor Mary Cassatt. In 1993, a major art show entitled "The Women Impressionists"—featuring Mary Cassatt's most important paintings and prints—attracted huge crowds at museums across Europe. Her reputation as an innovator, and as one of the best painters of her time, continues to grow. She was a person who did not choose the easy way. She could have lived a comfortable life among society families in Philadelphia, but instead devoted her life to reaching the high artistic standards she set for herself. She achieved them through her talent and intelligence, and, perhaps even more importantly, through hard work and perseverance.

Mary Cassatt, photographed at her country home in 1925, the year before she died

FOR FURTHER READING

Cain, Michael. *Mary Cassatt.* New York: Chelsea House, 1989.

Mary Cassatt (Video recording produced for WNET/13) Chicago: Homevision, 1977.

Meyer, Susan E. *Mary Cassatt.* New York: Abrams, 1990.

Turner, Robyn Montana. *Mary Cassatt: Portraits of Women Artists for Children.* Boston: Little, Brown, 1992.

Wilson, Ellen. *American Painter in Paris: A Life of Mary Cassatt.* New York: Farrar, Straus, 1971.

INDEX

ABOUT THE AUTHOR

Philip Brooks is a writer from Chicago, where he lives with his wife, Balinda. He received a master's degree in fiction writing from the University of Iowa, and his stories have appeared in various magazines. He is also the author of *Georgia O'Keeffe*, a biography for young readers published by Franklin Watts. Philip Brooks claims that he would rather be a painter, or a pro basketball player than a writer. Unfortunately, however, he can neither draw nor jump.